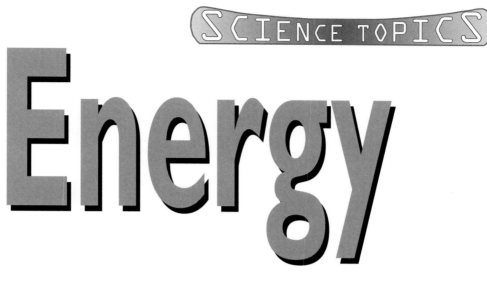

Energy

CHRIS OXLADE

Heinemann Library
Des Plaines, Illinois

Designed by AMR
Illustrations by Art Construction
Printed in Hong Kong

03 02 01 00 99
10 9 8 7 6 5 4 3 2 1

Oxlade, Chris
    Energy / Chris Oxlade.
       p. cm. – (Science topics.)
    Includes bibliographical references and index.
    Summary: Examines energy in its different forms, discussing heat
and temperature, changes of energy, alternative energy, and the role
of energy in supporting life.
    ISBN 1-57572-766-8 (library binding)
    1. Power resources—Juvenile literature. 2. Force and energy-
–Juvenile literature. [1. Power resources. 2. Force and energy.]
I. Title. II. Series.
TJ163.25.095. 1998
530—dc21   98-11587
                                   CIP
                                   AC

Acknowledgments
The Publishers would like to thank the following for permission to reproduce
photographs: Ann Ronan Picture Library pg. 5; Image Select/NOAA pg. 8, /NASA pgs. 9,
13, /Raleigh pg. 28; J. Allan Cash Ltd. pg. 7; Pix pg. 12, /L. Lefkowitz pg. 27; Planet
Earth/Wendy Dennis pg. 21; Science & Society Picture Library/Science Museum pg. 17;
Science Photo Library/David Parker pg. 11; Spectrum Color Library pg. 4; Tony Stone
Images/Mark Wagner pg. 23; Trevor Clifford pg. 19.

Cover photograph reproduced with permission of Image Select/NASA. Cover shows a
laser beam used in aerospace research over a background image of wind turbines.

Our thanks to Jane Taylor for her help in the preparation of this book.

Every effort has been made to contact copyright holders of any material reproduced in
this book. Any omissions will be rectified in subsequent printings if notice is given to the
Publisher.

Any words appearing in the text in bold, **like this**, are explained in the Glossary.

Contents

What is Energy?

Energy makes things happen. It makes plants grow, moves your bicycle when you pedal, makes computers work, pushes along huge locomotives, and makes wind blow and the rain fall. Whenever you see anything happening, energy is involved.

Imagine you are pushing a box along the floor. To make the box move along, you need to give it energy. You do this by pushing on the side of the box. When you stop pushing, you stop using energy. The energy you used pushing the box came from your muscles.

SCIENCE ESSENTIALS

There are many different forms of energy, and energy can change from one form to another. Energy is measured in **joules**. **Power** is measured in **watts**.

▼

In a big city, energy is used for transportation, for lighting, for heating, and for working machines in homes and offices.

Different forms of energy

We often think about the energy we use for heating, for lighting, and for making machines work in our homes, offices, and factories. This energy comes in the form of electricity and **fuels**. But energy can exist in many different forms. For example, all moving things have energy— electricity is a form of energy, heat is a form of energy, light is a form of energy, and sound is a form of energy. Energy can change from one form to another, just as electricity changes to light in a light bulb. In fact, whenever any event happens, energy is changing from one form to another.

Energy and power

Energy is measured in units called joules (J), named after the British physicist James Joule (1818–1889). One joule is not much energy. You use up a few hundred joules just getting out of bed, and it takes hundreds of thousands of joules to **boil** a kettle of water.

Power is how quickly energy is changed. Power is measured in watts (W). One watt is equal to one joule per second. This means that a 100 watt lightbulb changes or uses up 100 joules of electrical energy every second.

The power of horses

Most machines have a power rating in watts. For example, a hairdryer may be rated at 500 watts, to show that it uses 500 joules of **electrical energy** each second. However, engines and vehicles normally have a power rating in horsepower.

The unit of horsepower was invented in the late 1700s by British engineer James Watt. (The watt is named after him.) Watt was a pioneer of steam engines. He gave his engines a power rating so that people could compare their power to the power of a horse, which some of the engines were built to replace. One horsepower equals 746 watts.

▼

Early steam engines had very low horsepower.

Energy in Objects

When you make an object move, or you stretch or squash it, you use energy. The energy is transferred from you to the object. It is called mechanical energy. An object can have three types of mechanical energy—**kinetic energy, elastic energy**, and **gravitational energy**.

SCIENCE ESSENTIALS

Moving objects have kinetic energy. Gravitational energy is energy stored in an object because of its position in the earth's gravitational field. Bent, squashed, or stretched objects store elastic energy.

Energy in movement

Any object that is moving has a type of energy called kinetic energy. The faster an object moves and the heavier it is, the more kinetic energy it has. A force is needed to make an object start moving. Energy is needed to make that force. The longer the force is applied, the faster the object goes, and the more kinetic energy it gets. When an object slows, its kinetic energy reduces until it has none when it has stopped.

Elastic energy

One way of storing energy in an object is by bending, squashing, or stretching it. When you let the object go, it springs back into shape, releasing the energy again. This only works with materials which come back into shape when released, such as springs. These are called **elastic** materials. The energy stored in them is called elastic energy.

▲ As this pole-vaulter positions his pole, it bends, storing energy. When the pole straightens out, the energy is released, lifting the pole-vaulter up to the bar.

Higher and lower

An object does not have to be moving to have energy. Any object that could fall downward has energy, too. This sort of energy is called gravitational energy because the object is being pulled downward by the earth's **gravity**. The higher up an object is, and the heavier it is, the more gravitational energy it has. By moving an object upward against the force of gravity, you give it more gravitational energy. The energy you used is stored in the object and can be released later. Scientists often call this stored energy **potential energy**.

Flywheels

Spinning objects have movement or kinetic energy, too. A flywheel is a heavy disc, usually made of metal, that can spin. When it is spinning, it is a store of kinetic energy.

Many engines, such as steam engines, produce energy in short bursts. These bursts of energy are stored in a flywheel. The energy in the flywheel can then be released gradually, giving a smooth flow of energy from the engine. Imagine a flywheel made of many different segments—a bit like a dartboard. Each segment has kinetic energy because it is moving in a circle. Segments further from the center move faster and have more energy.

You can see the heavy, circular flywheel connected to this potter's wheel. The potter kicks the flywheel to keep it moving.

More Forms of Energy

Some forms of energy are easy to identify as energy. Other forms of energy cannot be seen until the energy is released. Some forms of energy, such as light and sound, carry energy from one place to another.

Energy in waves

Sound is made by vibrating objects, which have **kinetic energy**. The vibrations spread through the air in **waves**, carrying the energy with them. So, sound is a form of energy. The **particles** in the air vibrate as the sound waves go by, but do not actually move along. The louder the sound, the more energy there is in the vibrations of the particles.

Waves in the sea, and even in your bath, have energy in them, too. When a wave goes past, water does not move along, but just up and down. Energy moves through the water away from where the wave was caused, but the water does not move along itself. The higher the waves, the more energy there is in them.

As water and sound waves spread out from their source, the energy spreads out, too. This means that as you move away from the source, the amount of energy that reaches you decreases. For example, the further you get from the source of a sound, the quieter it seems.

This damage on the coast of Nicaragua was caused by a huge, energy-packed wave, 30 feet (9 meters) high, called a tidal wave, or tsunami.

Light energy

Light is also a form of energy. **Light energy** travels in straight lines called **rays**. A light ray carries energy from where the light is made. There is more energy in bright light than dim light. You can also think of light like waves. It spreads out, getting weaker as it does so.

This is why lights look dimmer the further away you get from them. Light is part of the family of rays called the **electromagnetic spectrum**. It includes radio waves, **microwaves**, heat rays, and X-rays. All these rays are forms of energy. This energy is often called **radiation**.

► A laser beam is an intense beam of light energy. This laser beam is making measurements during aerospace research.

Electrical energy

Electrical energy is a very useful form of energy because it can be sent along wires and used to work many different types of machines. (Find out about electricity in our homes on page 24.)

Chemical energy

Chemical energy is the energy stored in substances. We only see signs of this energy when the substance takes part in a chemical reaction.

For example, when a **fuel** burns, the chemical energy in it is released as heat and light energy. The energy stored in a **battery** is actually chemical energy.

When the battery is connected to an **electric circuit**, the energy is released as electrical energy.

Nuclear energy

Nuclear energy is the energy stored in the nucleus of an atom. When a nuclear reaction takes place, energy can be released as heat and light and other radiation, for example, X-rays.

Heat and Temperature

Everybody can feel the difference between hot and cold, but do you know why there is a difference? It has to do with another type of energy—**heat energy**. The tiny **particles** that make up substances are constantly moving or vibrating, but the particles and their movements are too small to see. The energy of these movements is heat energy.

SCIENCE ESSENTIALS

Heat is a form of energy. **Temperature** is a measure of how hot or cold a substance is. Temperature is measured in degrees **Fahrenheit** (°F) or **Celsius** (°C). Heat must be added to an object to raise its temperature. A large, cool object can have more heat energy than a small, hot object.

Hot or cold?

Every object has heat energy in it. If you add heat energy to an object, the particles move about more quickly. This makes the object feel hotter—its temperature is higher than before. If you take away heat energy, the particles move more slowly. This makes the object feel cooler—its temperature is lower than before. So, an object's temperature depends on how much its particles are moving.

The amount of heat energy in an object depends on the object's temperature and size. The hotter the object and the larger it is, the more heat energy it has. A large, cool object can have more heat energy than a small, hot object. For example, a lukewarm glass of water has more heat energy than a red-hot spark from a fireworks sparkler. The spark is far hotter, but has only a tiny amount of heat energy.

Cooling down

Heat energy always moves from hotter things to colder things. The bigger the difference in temperature between the two things, the faster the heat moves. The heat gradually spreads so that the temperature of both things becomes the same. For example, if you pour hot water into a cold mug, heat moves from the water to the mug until the temperature of the water and the mug is the same.

▼ This graph is called a cooling curve. It shows how a hot object cools in the air. It cools quickly at first and then more slowly.

As cold as it gets

You can keep adding heat energy to an object forever. The particles will vibrate more and more, and the object will get hotter and hotter. So there is no upper limit to temperature. But if you keep taking heat energy away from an object, the object will eventually run out of energy, and its particles will stop vibrating. It will reach a point at which it cannot get any colder. This happens at 0°**K** (− 459°F or −273°C). This temperature is called absolute zero because it is the lowest possible temperature. In the laboratory, scientists can only cool objects to within a few hundredths of a degree of absolute zero. It can never be reached because the last tiny piece of energy cannot be removed.

▼ Strange things happen at temperatures close to absolute zero. Some materials become super**conductors**, which means electricity can flow through them very easily. Here, an electric current is flowing around a superconductor all by itself, making a **magnetic field** that is keeping the magnet suspended.

Heat On the Move

Heat energy can move from one place to another. If something feels hot, it is because heat energy is moving from the object into your skin. If something feels cold, it is because heat energy is moving from your skin into the object.

Conducting heat

Heat energy can flow through a solid. This movement is called conduction. Inside the substance, heat energy is passed from one **atom** to the next. For example, when you put a cold metal spoon in a hot drink, heat from the drink flows into the spoon, making the bottom of the spoon warm. The heat then flows up the handle by conduction. Materials that conduct heat easily are called good **conductors**. Bad conductors are good **insulators**.

Rays of heat

Heat can also travel in **rays**, just as light does. This is called radiation. It is how the heat from the sun travels to the earth, and how heat reaches you from a glowing fire. Convection and conduction both need a substance to travel in, but radiation can travel through a **vacuum**. The heat rays are actually called **infra-red** rays. They are given off by all objects. The hotter the object, the stronger the rays are.

Our bodies are warm, so they also give off infra-red radiation. Emergency services sometimes use cameras which can detect infra-red to find people in dark or smoke-filled buildings.

When heat rays hit dark-colored objects, they are absorbed, making the object warmer. These houses are painted white so that heat rays bounce off, keeping them cool.

Heat swirls

Heat moves through liquids and gases by convection. If one part of the liquid or gas is heated, its atoms or **molecules** begin to move faster. This makes the liquid or gas **expand**, which makes it less dense. It floats upwards, carrying the heat energy with it and is replaced by cooler, denser liquid or gas. This movement of liquid or gas is called a convection current.

Terrific tiles

Materials that are bad conductors of heat (and therefore good insulators) are useful for giving protection against intense **temperatures**. Ceramics, such as glass, china, and brick, are all good insulators. As an object travels at great speed from space into the earth's atmosphere, friction between its surface and the air makes the object intensely hot—so hot that the object vaporizes. A space shuttle is protected from this heat by a layer of ceramic tiles. The outside surface of a tile reaches a temperature of more than 2,200°F (1,250°C), but because the heat cannot travel through the ceramic, the inside surface stays cool. This happens even though the tiles are only a couple of inches thick.

You can see the layer of heat-resistant tiles on the left of this photograph of a space shuttle in orbit.

Measuring Temperature

Temperature is usually measured in degrees, **Fahrenheit** (°F) or **Celsius** (°C). Measuring temperature accurately is important in medicine, engineering, manufacturing, and cooking. **Thermometers** are the instruments used to measure temperature.

SCIENCE ESSENTIALS

Temperature is measured in degrees Fahrenheit or Celsius. Temperature is measured with a thermometer.

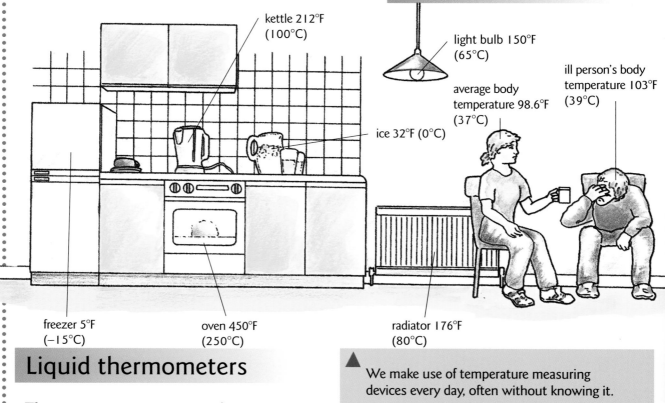

kettle 212°F (100°C)

light bulb 150°F (65°C)

ill person's body temperature 103°F (39°C)

average body temperature 98.6°F (37°C)

ice 32°F (0°C)

freezer 5°F (−15°C)

oven 450°F (250°C)

radiator 176°F (80°C)

We make use of temperature measuring devices every day, often without knowing it.

Liquid thermometers

The most common type of thermometer is the liquid thermometer. It consists of a small bulb full of liquid—usually alcohol or mercury—connected to a very narrow tube. As the temperature rises, the liquid in the bulb **expands**, and some moves along the tube. The higher the temperature, the more the liquid expands, and the further the liquid moves along the tube. There may be a liquid thermometer in a first aid kit, or in a greenhouse to measure the temperature of the room.

Alternative thermometers

We cannot use liquid thermometers to measure extremely hot or extremely cold temperatures. The liquid inside would either **freeze** or **boil**, and at very high temperatures, the glass would melt. Instead, we can use electronic thermometers, or **bimetallic strips**, which bend a different amount as the temperature changes.

Measuring body temperature

Doctors measure the temperature of our bodies with a clinical thermometer. It is very accurate, and measures temperatures from about 95°F to 105°F (35°C to 40°C). Normal body temperature is 98.6°F (37°C). You place a clinical thermometer under your tongue and wait for a few minutes until the liquid reaches the same temperature as your body. An alternative is the plastic strip thermometer that is placed on the forehead and changes color to indicate temperature.

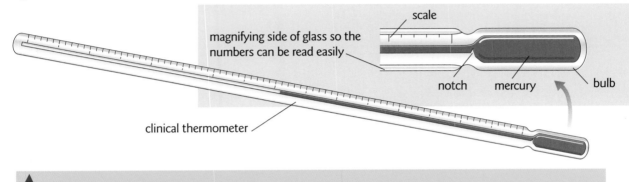

scale

magnifying side of glass so the numbers can be read easily

notch mercury bulb

clinical thermometer

▲ Because the liquid will cool and **contract** between the time the thermometer is removed from your mouth and the reading is taken, there is a narrow constriction in the tube of a clinical thermometer to stop the liquid from flowing back down.

Keeping a stable temperature

We often want to keep the temperature in an **environment** at the same level all the time. For example, the temperature in an oven needs to stay at the temperature set on the oven's controls.

This is done with a device called a thermostat. If the temperature rises too high, the thermostat tries to reduce it, and if the temperature falls too low, the thermostat tries to raise it.

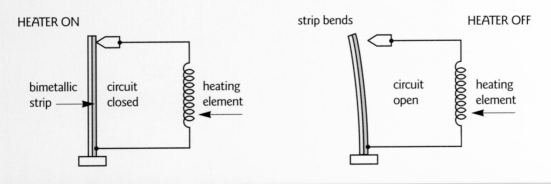

HEATER ON

bimetallic strip
circuit closed
heating element

strip bends
HEATER OFF

circuit open
heating element

▲ This is a simple thermostat—a device that keeps the temperature in a room or an oven steady. When the heating element is on, the temperature rises. The bimetallic strip bends, turning the element off by breaking (opening) the circuit.

Changes of Energy

You have seen that there are many different forms of energy, such as **kinetic energy**, **light energy**, and **heat energy**. Each form of energy can change to different forms of energy. Here are some examples of energy changes.

SCIENCE ESSENTIALS

The principle of conservation of energy is that energy cannot be created or destroyed. It can only be changed from one form into another. An energy transfer diagram shows how energy is transferred from one place to another.

Energy transfers

When you drop an object to the ground, its **gravitational energy** begins to turn to kinetic energy. The further the object falls, the more gravitational energy is converted, and the faster the object moves. As a **pendulum** swings, its energy is converted from gravitational to kinetic energy and then back again. (See page 18.) When a drummer hits a drum, the kinetic energy in the drumstick is converted into **sound energy**. In a loudspeaker, **electrical energy** is converted to sound.

Energy transfer diagrams

We can show how energy changes with a simple diagram. It shows how energy is transferred from one form to another, so it is called an energy transfer diagram. In many energy changes, two or more different types of energy are made. This can also be shown in an energy transfer diagram.

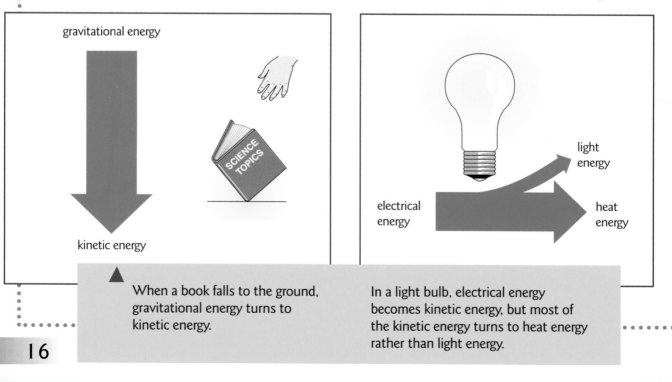

When a book falls to the ground, gravitational energy turns to kinetic energy.

In a light bulb, electrical energy becomes kinetic energy, but most of the kinetic energy turns to heat energy rather than light energy.

Conservation of energy

Energy sometimes seems to disappear, but it does not really do so. For example, some of the energy you use to ride a bicycle makes heat energy which you cannot see inside the bicycle's bearings. Heat energy is nearly always made during energy transfers, and is wasted because it leaks away into the air. (You can find out more about this on pages 28–29.) In fact, energy cannot be destroyed, and it cannot be created from nothing. It can only be changed from one form into another. This is called the principle of conservation of energy.

Useful electricity

Electrical energy can be changed easily into light energy, heat energy, and kinetic (or movement) energy. It can also be sent along wires and controlled by **electric circuits**. This makes it a very convenient form of energy, which is why it is used in homes, offices, and factories. (You can find out how electrical energy is made on pages 24–25.)

A wind-up radio

In many remote areas of the world, **batteries** are hard to find and very expensive. That is why British inventor Trevor Bayliss started work on his clockwork radio. His idea was to store energy in a spring, which would turn a small generator to make the electricity for the radio. At first, he could only store enough energy in the spring for a few minutes of sound. In the final model, which went on sale in 1994, a few seconds of winding the spring stores enough energy to keep the radio playing for 30 minutes.

▶ Turning the handle on the right puts energy into the radio. The energy comes out as sound energy!

Energy for Telling the Time

It is often useful to store energy so that we can use it later. Some clocks work with the help of electricity. Other clocks and watches don't need a store of energy to keep them working for days on end. Where does this energy come from? How is it stored inside the watch or clock? And how is it changed into the energy needed to make them work?

Falling weights

The first mechanical clocks were built in medieval times and had a heavy weight that gradually fell towards the floor. Cuckoo clocks and grandfather clocks work in the same way. The energy stored is **gravitational energy**. As the weight falls, it works the clock. The clock's mechanism releases the energy very slowly. When the weight reaches the floor, it must be raised again by hand. This only takes a few seconds, but it stores all the energy the clock needs to work for several days. Some ancient clocks used the energy in falling water instead of a weight.

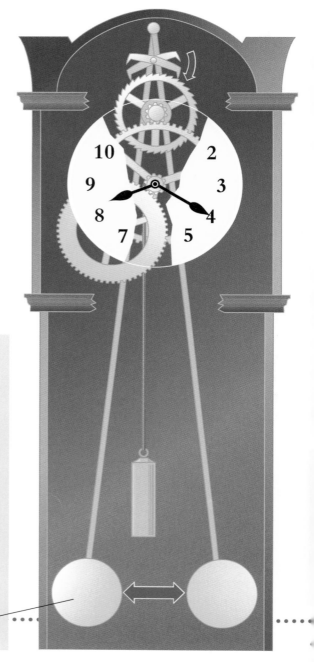

Each swing of a **pendulum** takes the same amount of time, so a pendulum can accurately control the speed of a clock.

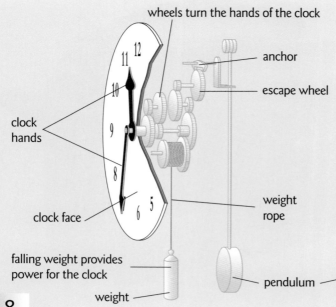

wheels turn the hands of the clock

anchor

escape wheel

clock hands

clock face

weight rope

falling weight provides power for the clock

weight

pendulum

Winding it up

Clocks and watches that you wind up every few days store energy in a spring. As you wind, the spring becomes more and more tightly coiled. The energy is stored as **elastic energy** in the spring. The mechanism in the watch gradually releases the energy in the spring, making the watch work for a few days before it needs to be rewound.

▶ Can you see the coiled spring of this clock on the left of the picture? The speed of the clock is controlled by a small wheel called a balance wheel, which spins one way and then the other—the same way a pendulum swings from side to side.

Battery power

Electric clocks and watches have a **battery** inside. This is where energy is stored as **chemical energy**. The energy is released as **electrical energy**, which works a tiny electric motor. The motor turns the mechanism inside the watch. Gradually, the chemicals in the battery are used up. When they run out, the battery must be replaced.

Digital clocks and watches do not have moving parts. The energy in the battery works the **electric circuits** inside the watch, and sometimes lights up the watch face which displays the time. Some electronic watches have a tiny **solar cell** that makes electricity from sunlight.

Watching your energy

Some watches get their energy from the movements of the wearer. As the person's wrist moves about, a small weight swings about inside the watch.

A special mechanism stores this **kinetic energy** so that it can be used to work the watch.

Energy for Life

Plants and animals are living things, and they need energy to live. Plants get the energy they need from sunlight. Animals, including humans, get their energy from the food they eat.

Sunlight for growth

All animals eat plants or other animals that eat plants. This means that all the energy animals need comes from plants in the first place. All the energy for plant and animal life on Earth comes from the sun. Plants do not need to search for food—most make their own.

Inside their leaves, light energy from the sun combines with water and **carbon dioxide** to make chemicals called carbohydrates. This process is called photosynthesis. The plant uses the carbohydrates to grow. Energy is stored as **chemical energy**.

SCIENCE ESSENTIALS
Plants get the energy to grow from sunlight.
Animals eat food to get the energy they need to live.
Different types of food have different amounts of energy stored in them.

Energy for animals

Animals eat food to get the energy they need to move and keep warm. The energy is stored in food in the form of chemical energy. When the food is eaten, the energy is stored in the body in chemicals. Our muscles convert the chemical energy to **kinetic energy** and **heat energy**.

Foods that contain carbohydrates, such as bread and pasta, are a good source of energy because the body can use the chemical energy in carbohydrates easily. Fatty foods have lots of energy, too. However, if you take in more energy than you use, the extra energy is stored as fat in your body. Too much fat is unhealthy.

Food contains other useful chemicals, too. For example, fruits and vegetables contain vitamins, proteins, and minerals. They contain hardly any energy, but they are vital to keep our bodies working properly. This is why it is important to eat a balanced diet.

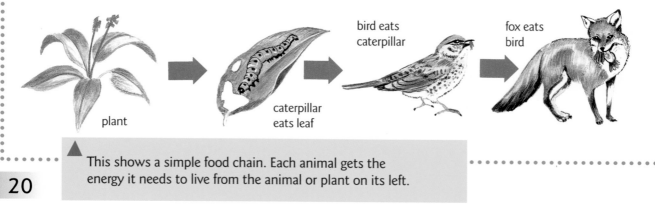

bird eats caterpillar

fox eats bird

plant

caterpillar eats leaf

This shows a simple food chain. Each animal gets the energy it needs to live from the animal or plant on its left.

How much energy?

The amount of energy stored in foods is often listed on food packaging. It is measured in kilocalories (kcal), commonly shortened to "calories." The figure given is usually the energy in every 100 grams of the food.

If you look at some food packages, you will see that some foods have much more energy than others. People who exercise need to eat high-energy food, such as pasta. Top athletes often eat a large meal of pasta a few hours before competing.

Warm and cold blood

Your body is always making heat energy from the energy you eat in food. This keeps you warm. On cold days, your body makes more heat to keep your **temperature** up. On hot days, your body makes less heat, and you sweat to help keep your temperature down. This is called being warm-blooded. All mammals and birds are warm-blooded.

Amphibians, reptiles, and fish are cold-blooded. Their bodies change temperature with their **environment**. Some cold-blooded animals change their body temperature by moving in and out of the sunlight.

▼
This lizard is basking in the morning sunshine to warm its body temperature before it goes hunting.

Burning for Energy

When something burns, **heat energy** is produced. It was stored in the material in the form of **chemical energy**. Burning changes the chemical energy into **heat energy**. It also makes some **light energy** at the same time. Burning is useful for heating and for lighting.

SCIENCE ESSENTIALS

Fossils **fuels** were formed millions of years ago. They trapped energy that came from the sun. Fossil fuels are non-renewable.

A chemical reaction

Burning happens when the chemicals in a substance combine with **oxygen**. There is a chemical reaction between the substance and the oxygen which releases the chemical energy stored in the substance. The reaction creates new chemicals, too. **Carbon dioxide** and water are made during burning.

Burning does not just start happening on its own. Some energy is needed to make the substance hot enough to burn in the first place. Once the burning has started, some of the energy made does the heating. The burning continues until all of the **fuel** is used up.

What is a fuel?

Any substance that we burn to make heat or light is called a fuel. Good fuels make lots of heat energy when they burn. There are two main types of fuel: biomass fuels and fossil fuels. Biomass fuels are plants, such as wood, which have grown recently. Biomass fuel is called a renewable fuel because new plants can be grown quite quickly to replace the ones that have been burned.

Fossil fuels include coal, oil, and gas. They are called fossil fuels because they are formed from the remains of plants and animals that lived on Earth hundreds of millions of years ago. Coal, oil, and gas are very efficient fuels. When they burn, they create twice as much energy as the same amount of wood. Fossil fuels are non-renewable fuels. Eventually they will run out.

▶ Three things are needed for burning to continue—fuel, heat, and oxygen. Fires can be tackled by removing one of these things. For example, covering a small fire with a blanket removes the oxygen and puts the fire out.

Burning problems

Burning fuels creates environmental problems. Carbon dioxide from burning is being released into the atmosphere where it traps the sun's heat. This is called the **greenhouse effect**. As carbon dioxide builds up in the atmosphere, more and more heat is trapped.

In turn, the earth's atmosphere is gradually warming up. This is called **global warming**. Most fuels create other chemicals when they burn, too, such as sulphur dioxide and soot which is mostly carbon. These chemicals can cause **acid rain** and **smog**.

Solving the problems?

There are two ways of reducing the amount of carbon dioxide in the atmosphere. The first way is to cut down carbon dioxide produced by burning fuels. This can be done by reducing the amount of fuel burned and by making engines and **power stations** more efficient. The second way is to stop cutting down forests, where trees and other plants take in carbon dioxide as they grow. (See page 20.)

Unfortunately, this may not be as easy to achieve as it sounds. In industrialized countries, cutting carbon dioxide emissions would mean a loss of jobs. In many other countries, tree-cutting is the best source of income and a way of life for farmers.

► Airplanes are a source of pollution as they leave trails of carbon dioxide and unburned fuel in the air.

Making Electricity

Electrical energy is a very convenient form of energy to use in our homes, offices, and factories. Electircal energy is easy to move from place to place and can be turned into many different forms of energy, such as **light energy**, **heat energy**, and **kinetic energy**. Imagine what it would be like without all the electrical machines and gadgets around your house and school.

Electric generators

If you have seen a bicycle with a generator instead of **batteries** to work its lights, you might know how electricity is made. The generator is a device that makes electrical energy from kinetic energy. It looks like an electric motor. Spinning its shaft makes it produce electrical energy. On a bicycle, the generator is turned by one of the wheels, but the energy comes from your legs! And of course, the lights go out when the bicycle stops.

Most of the electricity we use at home and at school is made by huge generators in power stations. The electricty travels away from the power station along thick cables supported on tall towers. As the cables get nearer where the electricity is used, they divide up into smaller cables or wires that go to each house or factory. These cables are either underground or strung on poles.

Beware – high voltage!

You probably know that high overhead power lines are very dangerous because of their high **voltage**. But why do they have voltages of hundreds of thousands of volts when the voltage in our homes is only 220 volts? The answer is that it saves energy. When an electric **current** flows in a cable, it makes the cable warm, so some of the electrical energy is changed to heat. This heats the air around the cable and is wasted. The stronger the current, the more heat is lost. The same amount of energy can be sent along the cable by increasing the voltage and reducing the current. This reduces the heat loss.

Energy in a power station

At a coal-fired power station, the **chemical energy** stored in the coal is turned into electrical energy. This energy change cannot happen at once. A generator is needed to make the electricity, so the chemical energy must be converted to kinetic energy to work the generator.

This is done by burning the coal to make heat energy, using the heat energy to **boil** water to make steam, and using the steam to make a **turbine** spin around. Less than half of the chemical energy becomes electrical energy. The rest is lost in the power station.

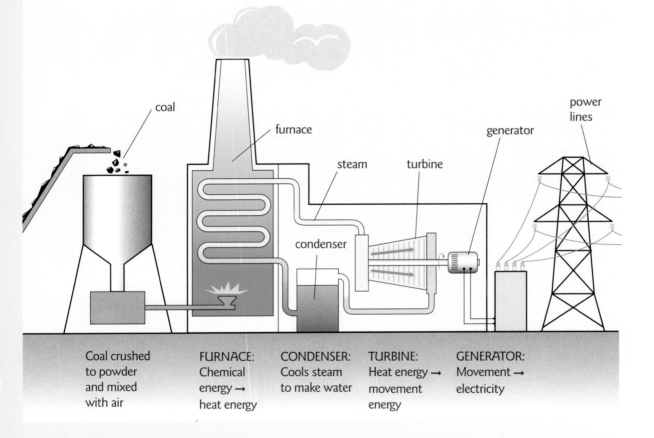

| Coal crushed to powder and mixed with air | FURNACE: Chemical energy → heat energy | CONDENSER: Cools steam to make water | TURBINE: Heat energy → movement energy | GENERATOR: Movement → electricity |

▲ This is the layout of machinery in a typical coal-fired power station. The coal is crushed into powder to make it burn more efficiently. It is burned in a furnace, where it heats water to make steam.

The steam rushes through the turbine, making it spin, and then the steam condenses to water again. The turbine spins the generator, and towers and power lines carry the electricity to where it is needed.

Alternative Energy

Alternative energy is energy used for home and industry made by sources other than burning **fuels.** These alternative forms of energy do not make **greenhouse gases** or poisonous pollutants. They are also all renewable forms of energy.

Some alternative forms of energy, such as wind power, are not new. They have been used for thousands of years. In some parts of the world, alternative energies are plentiful. For example, in wet, mountainous countries, water power is frequently used. In other parts of the world, there may be no choice but to burn fuels.

Energy in the wind

Wind is moving air, and although air is very light, even a light wind has lots of **kinetic energy** in it. Winds are actually **convection** currents caused by the Sun heating up the air in the earth's atmosphere.

A wind **turbine** collects the energy in the wind. In a traditional windmill, the energy turns machinery for grinding grain or for pumping water. A modern turbine turns a generator that turns the kinetic energy into **electrical energy**.

Energy in water

Water in rivers has energy, too. There is kinetic energy in flowing water, and **gravitational energy** in water stored behind a dam. In a water mill, the energy is used to make machinery work. At a hydroelectric **power station**, the flowing water turns an electricity generator to make electrical energy. A large hydroelectric station can produce as much power as a similar-sized, coal-fired power station.

Tidal power stations capture the energy in sea water as it flows in and out as the tide rises and falls. There have also been experiments in capturing the energy in sea **waves**.

Energy under the ground

In some places on Earth, especially near volcanoes, there are hot rocks quite near the surface. These rocks can heat water that is pumped into the ground. The warm water can be used for heating homes and offices. This sort of energy is called geothermal energy.

Catching energy from the sun

A huge amount of **heat energy** from the sun hits the earth. Some arrives as light, some as heat, and some as other sorts of electromagnetic **rays**, such as ultra-violet. This energy is called **solar energy**. One way of capturing solar energy is with a solar panel on the roof of a building. When the sun shines on the panel, it heats water inside pipes which flow through the panel. The hot water is used for heating and washing. **Solar cells** use special chemicals to turn **light energy** into electrical energy. They are used on some electronic devices, such as watches and calculators. (See page 19.)

And now the bad news . . .

Alternative energy sources do not create the environmental problems that fossil fuels do, but they do create their own problems. One of the main ones is the size that the generating stations have to be to generate a useful amount of power. For example, a wind-generating farm needs several hundred individual turbines. The farm needs to be in a hilly area where plenty of wind is available, and this is likely to be in an area of natural beauty, where the farm can spoil the landscape.

Hydroelectric schemes also create problems. Building a large dam creates a huge reservoir upstream, drowning habitats. The dam itself stops animals moving up and down the river. Downstream, the natural flow of the river is disrupted, which can cause the river bed to fill up with silt.

Hilltop wind farms like this can be an eyesore. They also make a low humming noise, which some people say upsets cattle.

Losing Energy

Energy is valuable stuff! Whenever you listen to your stereo, switch on a light, turn on a heater, or travel in a car or bus, you use energy. And every time we use energy from fossil **fuels**, we are using up energy resources that are in limited supply. This means that it is important not to waste energy. The easiest way to save energy is to switch off anything we are not using. The other way is to use energy more efficiently.

SCIENCE ESSENTIALS

Some energy is always wasted because it turns to heat. **Insulation** reduces the amount of **heat energy** lost from a building.
Recycling saves energy.

Energy efficiency

When we change energy from one form to another, unwanted forms of energy are often made. For example, the job of a light bulb is to turn **electrical energy** into **light energy**. But only 5 percent of the electrical energy actually turns into light. The other 95 percent turns to unwanted **heat energy**. You can see that normal light bulbs are very inefficient at their job. Special energy-efficient light bulbs are better, but not perfect. They convert 25 percent of the electrical energy they use into light.

Energy is lost in all machines. The job of a car engine is to turn the **chemical energy** stored in fuel into **kinetic energy** of the car. Some of the energy is converted to heat, making the engine hot. More energy must be used to work a cooling system to stop the engine overheating. The engine also makes unwanted **sound energy**.

We also make unwanted heat when we exercise. The heat is created in our muscles as they convert chemical energy into kinetic energy. We have to sweat to get rid of the heat.

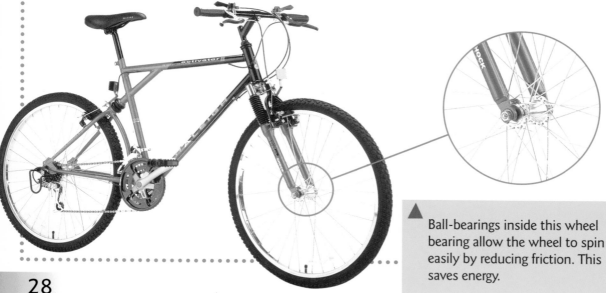

▲ Ball-bearings inside this wheel bearing allow the wheel to spin easily by reducing friction. This saves energy.

Friction and heat

When your hands are cold, you rub them together to warm them up. An energy change takes place: movement energy of your hands turns into heat energy. This is caused by friction between your hands. In any machine with moving parts, friction wastes energy by creating unwanted heat.

Recycling energy

We recycle materials, such as glass, paper, and aluminum. When we recycle, we are not throwing away the materials, and we do not need to find the raw materials to make more. But just as importantly, recycling saves the energy that would otherwise be used to process the raw materials.

Leaking heat

A huge amount of energy is wasted, especially during the winter when heat energy leaks out of houses and offices and into the atmosphere. Energy does not just leak through open windows and doors, but through the roof, the walls, and glass, by **convection** and **conduction**. The amount of energy that escapes can be reduced with double panes of glass and other sorts of **insulation** and draft-proofing.

A *never-ending problem*

For hundreds of years, inventors have of building a machine which would ke working forever once it was started, any more energy being added. This id called perpetual motion. We now kno that perpetual motion is impossible to achieve because friction always turns some of the kinetic energy in the machine into heat energy, which leaks into the atmosphere.

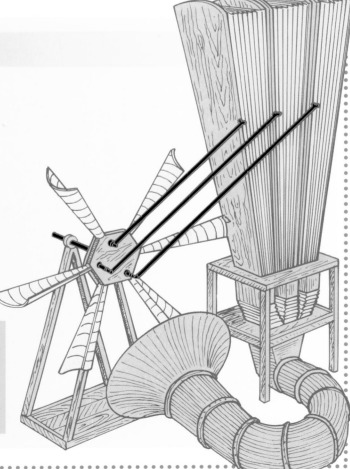

▶ Here's an example of a perpetual motion machine. The windmill operates the bellows, which make the wind to turn the windmill. However, this machine does not work. Why?

Glossary

acid rain   rain that becomes slightly acidic because it mixes with polluting gases in the atmosphere. Acid rain can eventually kill trees and water creatures in the areas where it falls

atom   the smallest particle of a substance that can exist. Atoms are the building blocks of all substances

battery   a store of chemicals that release their energy as electricity when connected to an **electric circuit**

bimetallic strip   a strip made up of two pieces of different metals joined together. As the **temperature** rises, the metals **expand** at a different rate, which makes the strip bend

boil   to turn from liquid to gas

carbon dioxide   a gas that is present in the atmosphere in tiny amounts, but which is vital for plant life

Celsius (°C)   the **SI unit** of **temperature** on which the freezing point of water is 0°

chemical energy   the energy stored in chemicals that can be released when the chemical takes part in a chemical reaction

conduction   the movement of heat through solid objects. The energy is passed from **atom** to atom

conductor   a material that allows electricity or heat to flow through it easily

contract   to get smaller

convection   the movement of energy through a liquid or gas because the liquid or gas circulates (moves around)

current   a flow of electricity, made up of electrons moving inside an electrical **conductor**

elastic   describes a material that returns to its original shape after the force stretching, squashing, or bending it has been removed

elastic energy   the energy stored in a squashed, stretched or bent **elastic** object

electric circuit   a loop of material that **conducts** electricity which an electric current can flow around

electrical energy   the energy carried by an **electric current** flowing around a circuit

electromagnetic spectrum   a family of similar **waves**, including light, radio waves, **microwaves** and X-rays

environment   a living thing's surroundings

expand   to get larger

Fahrenheit (°F)   a unit of **temperature** on which the freezing point of water is 32°

freeze   to turn from liquid to solid

fuel   a substance that is burned to produce useful energy, such as coal or petrol

global warming   the warming of the atmosphere caused by the **greenhouse effect**

gravitational energy   the potential energy that an object has because of its position in a gravitational field. On Earth, the higher up an object is, the more gravitational energy it has.

gravity   the force that pulls all objects with mass towards all other objects with mass

greenhouse effect   the trapping of the Sun's heat in the atmosphere caused by the increase of **greenhouse gases**

greenhouse gases   gases that trap the Sun's heat in the atmosphere, warming it up. The main greenhouse gas is **carbon dioxide.**

heat energy   the energy that an object has because of its **temperature**. Hotter, larger objects have more heat energy

infra-red   invisible **rays** similar to red light rays which carry **heat energy** from place to place

insulation   material used to stop electricity or heat escaping

insulator   a material that does not allow electricity or heat to flow through it

joule (J)   the **SI unit** of energy

K Kelvin, a measure of temperature like Farenheit or Celsius

kinetic energy the energy that an object has because it is moving or spinning round

light energy the energy carried from place to place in **rays** of light

magnetic field the region around a magnet where its magnetic effect can be felt

microwave a type of radio **wave** that can be aimed accurately and carries a lot of energy

molecule the smallest **particle** of a substance that normally occurs. It is usually made up of two or more **atoms** joined together

nuclear energy the energy stored inside an **atom**, which is released when the atom's nucleus (central part) splits up or combines with another nucleus

oxygen a gas of the atmosphere that animals need to breathe to live

particles microscopically small pieces of a substance, such as **molecules** in the air

pendulum a weight on the end of a string or rod that swings from side to side. Each swing of a pendulum takes the same amount of time, no matter how far it is swinging

potential energy energy that can be released by an object or a substance, such as **gravitational energy**, **elastic energy**, or **chemical energy**

power the rate at which energy is converted from one form to another

power station a place where electricity is made

radiation energy that travels in the form of electromagnetic **waves**, such as **infra-red** light

ray a beam of energy that travels in a straight line, such as light

SI unit a unit of measurement in the SI System of units (Système International d'Unités), which is used by scientists in most parts of the world

smog fog caused by smoke and other pollutants trapped in the atmosphere

solar cell a device that turns the **light energy** that falls on it into **electrical energy**

solar energy energy from the Sun, collected by solar panels or solar cells

sound energy vibrations that travel through the **particles** of the air, liquids or solids, carrying energy with them

temperature a measure of how hot an object is. Adding **heat energy** to an object increases its temperature

thermometer a device for measuring **temperature**

turbine a machine that is turned by a force, such as liquid or gas, flowing through it

vacuum a space that contains nothing, including air

voltage the potential energy that pushes a **current** around an **electric circuit**

watt (W) the **SI unit** of power, equal to one **joule** per second

waves vibrations of **particles** that carry energy from place to place, such as waves in water and sound waves in air, liquids, and solids

More Books to Read

Amdur, Richard. *The Fragile Earth*. New York: Chelsea House Publishers. 1994.

Lafferty, Peter. *The World of Science*. New York: Facts on File. 1994.

Index